SOMETHING SMALL OF HOW TO SEE A RIVER

Recent and Selected Titles from Tupelo Press

Nebulous Vertigo Belle Ling

Cyborg Fever Leslie Sheck

Westminster West Chard de Niord

Jalousie Allyson Paty

Mycocosmic Lesley Wheeler

Phantom Number: An Abecedarium for April Spring Ulmer

The Last Milkweed Alan Berolzheimer, Jeffrey Levine, & Allison O'Keefe, eds.

The Haunting Cate Peebles

The Radiant Lise Goett

The Opening Ritual G.C. Waldrep

The Right Hand Christina Pugh

Called Back Rosa Lane

Landsickness Leigh Lucas

Green Island Liz Countryman

The Beautiful Immunity Karen An-hwei Lee

Small Altars Justin Gardiner

Country Songs for Alice Emma Binder

Asterism Ae Hee Lee

then telling be the antidote Xiao Yue Shan

Therapon Bruce Bond & Dan Beachy-Quick

membery Preeti Kaur Rajpal

How To Live Kelle Groom

Sleep Tight Satellite Carol Guess

THINE Kate Partridge

The Future Will Call You Something Else Natasha Sajé

Night Logic Matthew Gellman

The Unreal City Mike Lala

Wind—Mountain—Oak: Poems of Sappho Dan Beachy-Quick

Tender Machines J. Mae Barizo

Best of Tupelo Quarterly Kristina Marie Darling, Ed.

We Are Changed to Dear at the Broken Place Kelly Weber

Why Misread a Cloud Emily Carlson

The Strings Are Lightning and Hold You In Chee Brossy

Ore Choir: The Lava on Iceland Katy Didden and Kevin Tsang

The Air in the Air Behind It Brandon Rushton

The Future Perfect: A Fugue Eric Pankey

American Massif Nicholas Regiacorte

City Scattered Tyler Mills

Today in the Taxi Sean Singer

April at the Ruins Lawrence Raab

The Many Deaths of Inocencio Rodrigue Iliana Rocha

The Lantern Room Chloe Honum

Love Letter to Who Owns the Heavens Corey Van Landingham

Inventory of Doubts Landon Godfrey

Glass Bikini Kristin Bock

Bed Elizabeth Metzger

Inventory of Doubts Landon Godfrey

Tension : Rupture Cutter Streeby, paintings Michael Haight

Afterfeast Lisa Hiton

Lost, Hurt, or in Transit Beautiful Rohan Chhetri

Glyph: Graphic Poetry=Trans. Sensory Naoko Fujimoto

The Pact Jennifer Militello

Nemerov's Door: Essays Robert Wrigley

"*Something Small* is an offering; a collection of poems that together reads as an epic poem and ode to all the water protectors at Standing Rock. Not the interlopers or spectators, but those who came to work in the name of our collective liberation. Throughout the poems, Teresa's voice is genuine, poignant, and unpretentious—putting words to memories and feelings that ordinarily defy them. It's a rare and exquisite talent to unflinchingly capture the beauty and violence of movement spaces—from the police dogs and water cannons to busy kitchens and children's songs—the poems journey us through the sights and sounds of the small, intimate moments that are often lost to the (made) spectacle of Standing Rock. In so doing, Teresa not only teaches us 'how to see a river,' but peels back the colonialist residue from the Mni Sosi, revealing a glimpse into all the life and beauty she sustains."

— Sandy Grande, author of *Red Pedagogy*

"In bracing, enlivening poems, Teresa Dzieglewicz makes her impressive debut as a poet of place and heart. Recounting her time spent with Lakȟóta and Dakota activists on the Standing Rock Reservation organizing against the Dakota Access Pipeline, *Something Small of How to See a River* fills in the gaps left by media's imperfect reporting—Dzieglewicz zeros in on the humanity at stake, and the hard and sometimes joyous mechanics at work (and play) in the fight for survival. I felt changed by this book."

— Lynn Melnick, author of *I've Had to Think Up a Way to Survive*

"*Something Small of How to See a River* sings in the dark. While reading this stunning collection, I was reminded of the quote by June Jordan, which states that 'Poetry is a political act because it involves telling the truth.' Teresa Dzieglewicz weaves her witnessing with devastating facts and stunning imagery. The personal collides with the political while tracking the 'slow waltz of survival" with innovative approaches to poetic form as the speaker reckons with the history and violence of land and language. I was captivated by these poems that reminded me of ceremony, beauty, and the depth of human connection amidst the terror, because as Dzieglewicz writes, '. . . maybe this is the most human thing we do: look upward, together, as the light changes from green to pink, the aurora wringing all these colors from the dark.'"

— Tiana Clark, author of *I Can't Talk about the Trees without the Blood*

SOMETHING SMALL OF HOW TO SEE A RIVER

POEMS

Teresa Dzieglewicz

Something Small of How to See a River

Library of Congress Control Number: 2022950001

ISBN-13: 978-1-946482-82-2

Cover and text design by Josef Beery.

Cover art: Original embroidery by Val Eagle Shield. Used by kind permission of the artist.

First paperback edition October 2025

Tupelo Press
P.O. Box 1767
North Adams, Massachusetts 01247
(413) 664-9611 / Fax: (413) 664-9711
editor@tupelopress.org / www.tupelopress.org

Tupelo Press is an award-winning independent literary press that publishes fine fiction, non-fiction, and poetry in books that are a joy to hold as well as read. Tupelo Press is a registered 501(c)(3) nonprofit organization, and we rely on public support to carry out our mission of publishing extraordinary work that may be outside the realm of the large commercial publishers. Financial donations are welcome and are tax deductible.

For the kids, always.

Table of Contents

CONFLUENCE

Foreword

In early 2016, a group of young people from the Očhéthi Šakówiŋ tribes—comprised of the Lakȟóta, Dakȟóta, and Nakȟóta people—began organizing in opposition to the construction of the Dakota Access Pipeline (DAPL). The 1,172 mile pipeline, designed to transport up to 570,000 gallons of fracked oil a day, was originally planned to run north of the predominantly white city of Bismark, ND. But after outcry from Bismarck residents about the risk of water contamination, the pipeline was re-routed to cross the Missouri River less than a mile upstream of the Standing Rock Reservation. This revised route threatened the sole water source for the Standing Rock and Cheyenne River reservations, and crossed land recognized by the treaties of 1851 and 1868, as well as numerous sites of significant cultural, historical, and spiritual value to the people of the Očhéthi Šakówiŋ.

The youth- and Indigenous-led movement opposing the construction of the pipeline centered on several camps near the pipeline route, including the Sacred Stone Camp and the Očhéthi Šakówiŋ Camp. By September, the Očhéthi Šakówiŋ Camp had a population of 7,000-10,000 people, with representatives from over 300 tribal nations. It was the largest gathering of Indigenous people in over one hundred years. At its peak, the Očhéthi Šakówiŋ Camp had several public kitchens, bi-weekly garbage collection, a regular porta-potty service, a donations center, and on-site medical, media, and legal teams, as well as school.

I first came to Standing Rock in August of 2016. I grew up in Chicago, as a third-generation immigrant of Italian and Polish descent. And although this was not my first time on a L/Dakȟóta reservation—I had been lucky enough to teach incredible students on Rosebud Reservation for three years—it was my first time visiting Standing Rock. I believed (and believe) strongly in the issues of sovereignty and environmental justice and I was planning to come up for a few days to bring donations.

Instead, I was lucky enough to meet Alayna Eagle Shield and to be introduced to Mní Wičhóni Nakíčižiŋ Owáyawa (Defenders of the Water School). Alayna founded the Owáyawa in late August at the prompting of families and elders who wished to educate kids at the camp within the movement and their own culture. Along with Alayna, Blaze Starkey, José Zhagñay, Savannah Begay, and Steve Tamayo,

I helped to co-direct the school and create a place for kids to learn from elders and community members. Our efforts continue today, with the goal of creating a long-term Lakȟóta and movement-based learning space (now called Mni Wičhóni Nakíčižiŋ Wóuŋspe) for Standing Rock.

This is only my small corner of the story. There is much I do not know and cannot tell, and I strongly urge you to seek out the voices of the many Indigenous writers (including Natalie Diaz, Jennifer Foerster, Elizabeth Sweetly, Mark Tilsen, Louise Erdrich, Heid Erdrich, Craig Santos-Perez, and Layli Long Soldier), artists (including Ricardo Caté, Steve Tamayo, Jackie Fawn, and Christi Belcourt), musicians (including Raye Zaragoza and Scatter Their Own), journalists (including the late Myron Dewey, Desiree Cane, and the Indigenous Environmental Network), movement leaders (including the late Joye Braun, Waniya Locke, the Standing Rock Youth Council, and Faith Spotted Eagle), and academics (including Alayna Eagle Shield, Nick Estes, Sandy Grande, and the Stand with Standing Rock committee) whose work tells this necessary story.

Note: There are a number of different orthographies, or spelling systems, for the Lakȟóta language. I've chosen to use the writing system used by Mní Wičhóni Nakíčižiŋ Wóuŋspe, which was developed by Lakȟóta educator, writer, and linguist Ella Deloria.

✳ *Indicates state violence.*

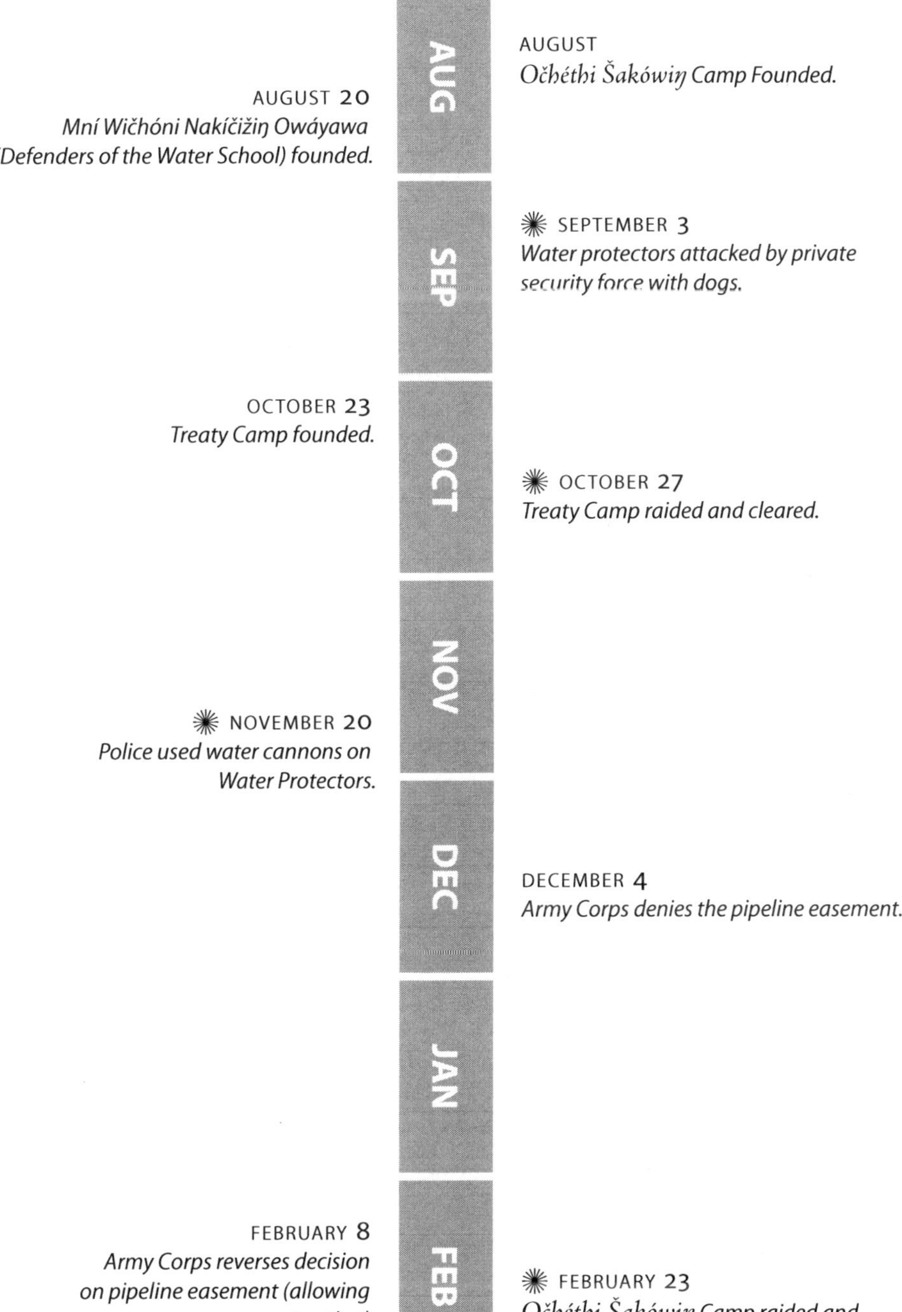

August at Očhéthi, One Year Later

Crawl beyond barbed wire. Stand in the place you stood
            where you burned your fingers on the barely-live

embers of the Sacred Fire's final night, looked
            at the half-abandoned world you'd loved; torn

snow pants, ice-crisped thípi, brittle hay;
            wondered if anything would feel as alive

again. All year you've failed to unremember the dwindling
            firewood, helicopters scrawling contusions into sky.

But, the drifts of snow that swelled shut the door
            of the yurt are now groundwater, keep alive

the roots of the wood lily and blazing star. The state
            can take but not erase the hooves that spoke small o's

along the dirt, or the log the kids climbed, hemmed now
            in clover. And I'm here again, touching my own life

lines to the Cannonball, open-palmed, ready to sift the silt, see
            this river snail beside my skin, the small home-making

of the caddis flies. *Teresa, you are water too.* And though
            the river is not untouched, still, it squalls with life.

HEADWATERS

I went to the camp first in the very beginning, in the first month, wouldn't that be April? There were maximum 80 people, not very much. I didn't really think it was going to take off. All of a sudden, come back a month or two later and literally thousands of people were there and you had to wait car after car after car to get in or even find a spot. After that, literally everyone knew each other because we were all crammed into the area. I couldn't believe this was all happening at my home.

HALLE MARTINEZ

age 18 (age 14 at camp)

Tonight, I Haven't Even Said the Word Pipeline

I peel the tape off these boxes with Alayna; open
    their mouths that sing with gifts of seed beads,
neon scissors, fat-shimmered spools of sinew. We garland
    this torn army tent with August corn; say *school* but mean *river,*

milkweed, clay. We say *everything is beginning*
    to arrive! Since the suspension of construction, for me,
there is only this tent flap, lifting; the kids' hands, plate-filled; small suns
    of yellow squash. The ridge where we carry our dinner; new power

streaming from solar panels, swelling the sound of the round dance.
    And see? Elders sipping soup. Toddlers wobbly with lightsabers
gift of sage scenting their t-shirts. Before we have to talk about tear gas
    and torn-down homes, give me this moment again, the rippling circles

of tents like jewel-toned fish, votives of thípis flickering
    across the prairie. Someone says *look* and we turn now,
toward the bright kernels of stars spread along the tarp
    of the sky. Follow my eyes and—see, there—tipping green

the poles of the thípis; drenching the night in fuchsia scarves;
    peeling and curling like birchbark from the Milky Way
—the Northern Lights. And in this second of hushed
    and held breath, I know there's so much I don't know

about the solar winds, disturbances storming beneath all of this
    beauty. But maybe this is the most human thing we do:
look upward, together, as the light changes from green to pink,
    the aurora wringing all these colors from the dark.

Learning the Plum Pit Game

1) You don't know the rules yet. Sit with the kids in this circle of grass. Listen.

(You see the smooth brome and want to say untouched. *Or soft as a child's head in your lap*. Don't. Even grasses have a history you don't understand.)

2) You have a partner and an opposing team. Take five plum pits, painted on one side, some with the tiniest buffalo, others with the winging of birds.

(These stalks planted here as forage for cattle who were planted in place of buffalo when they were turned to bleached planets of skull.)

3) Your turn: hold these plum pits in the palm of your hand. Shake them like dice. Feel the hoof trying to escape. The beak.

(Roots of native grass hold carbon in crenellated shapes fourteen feet underground. We are held here by castles.)

4) Flick your wrist, open your palm. The kids chant "tȟatȟáŋka, tȟatȟáŋka, tȟatȟáŋka" or "zitkála, zitkála"

(and in the hills beyond here, a bulldozer turns the land like the tossed dreams of fever, and the gasses rise like ghosts of the bluestem, the false boneset while)

5) You count your matches and mark your points and

(you are suspended in the palm of the prairie)

6) the amber wings of the Dakota Skipper disappear.

The Naming of Facebook Hill

Ricardo, camp cartoonist, pops the held breath
from a bag of hot cheetos, leans against his tangerine
pick-up, "Did I tell you about the hill?" his cigarette
lets loose neat packages of smoke.

I'm propped in the jaw
of my pontiac's hatchback, eating breakfast:
peanut butter straight from the heat-softened jar,
stale water chugged from gallon jugs. Still trying not to rely

on anyone: I've spent the morning drifting, like an empty
soda bottle on a river. If the Main Circle were an egg, the Fire
the rich yolk at the center, I orbited the laced and burnt
bits at its edge, knowing nobody, catching only
scraps of prayer.

I lick the plastic knife, shake my head.
It was when he'd just got here. It was mostly
Native people then, he says, before everybody else
started showing up. And he woke one morning—
5am, with the songs and the prayers and the women
all going down to the river,
all of that, just in that spiritual mode,

ya know? From his pick-up bed, he saw the silhouette
of an old man praying on the tallest hill. The one
that edges the road? Barbed rancher fence stuck in its side?
The man just looked, well, majestic, he tells me—
in that orange sunrise, arms circling his head
and angled toward that last leftover slice of moon.

ARRESTS TO DATE: 29

The cartoonist wanted to pray too, he tells me,
and so, headed uphill, through high grass, past tents
snoring with families, tarped cookshacks beginning
to boil with oatmeal.

The silhouette kept pacing the peak. Here,
Ricardo stops to mime how the man's hands
were clutched together and waving, how he spun
slow in back and forth semi-circles: some sort of dance, holy
in unrecognizable ways. He tells me as he got
closer the man's hands began

glowing. The edges of some item firmed to black
plastic. And then he saw it. Cracked screen.
Blue webpage. Heard the tiny tap dance
of buttons, the click of a sunrise selfie.

"All that time, I thought 'he's so holy,'
and he was just looking for service!"

The cartoonist reaches between our cars, offers
me the bag of hot cheetos,
and I take them, this small kindness
tingling in my throat. How easy it is to misunderstand what glows
in each of our hands and who am I to say

all of this is anything but holy,
the peanut butter I find later
on the edge of my cheek,
our fingers bright with small sunrises
of processed cheese, the old man's
portrait against the ink-smudged sky,
even the sharp fissures
in the cracks of his screen?

The Story Starts Like This: with Scraps of Shell

and the river, just beginning to chisel her bed across the not-yet
prairie, to score through prehistoric fangs of cats, sea-glass

smooth ribs of swept-away mammals. No nation dams her
yet, floods the homes along her banks, corners her in puny

lakes. No, now, she sows and sows. The once-hinged hull
of a mussel. A limpet emptied of its triangular heart. And new

mineral starts to cling, spends centuries swelling globe-like
and resistant around this swallowed archive. Now, weathering:

polishing away shale banks, revealing the shapes, up to ten feet
in diameter. In Lakȟota, this place is called the Íŋyaŋwakağapi Wakpá,

or Sacred Stone River. But when the soldiers came, saw the sun-lit
stones, warm and breathy as eggs, they re-christened her

the *Cannonball*: because when destiny means only more and more,
when all your tools are weapons, even a river starts to look like a war.

"If You're Married, Why Do You Call Her Teresa?"

Cheri asks, rehearsing fancy shawl, small arms like maple seeds,
pulling her into pirouette. Our tent stretches like a calf in the cattails,
"What should I call her?" Noah asks, expanding the center pole

into my hands. Only yesterday, I hiked the hill to call
and say, "I miss you. They need lawyers. Come now."

"Chee, call her Wife!" Bella scoffs. We laugh and the body
of our tent wobbles up, footprint obscuring tufts of seeding
grass. Beneath the girls' feet, butterflies, communion-thin,

steam from the land. And why don't we do this in English?
Name by relationship? When I crouch in the stomped dirt

circling the Sacred Fire, dinner propped on my knees, the kids yell
"Teacher!" This one word, a reminder of who I am. And I am ashamed
to say I am jealous sometimes. Of this land, its goldenrod

flinting the prairie dusk, the word "ancestral," which never belongs
like a plum on my tongue. I come from the body of a woman

I've never met, call only *biological*. Her helixes map a tangle
of wildflowers inside me, or rocky river's edge that I will never
name. Across gravel, the strong arms of women

stir blueberries down to their sweetest syrups, wóžapi
sugaring the air. I try and still am afraid to name this

relationship, what it means to be me, to be white on this
land, to settle my tent by the river I've been taught to call
Cannonball. How badly some nights, I want to call all of this

home. The girls run off to start a tea stand, sell the kitchen's wares
to dreadlocked weekenders. And I think, whenever I say "husband,"

I also say "my." We unroll our sleeping bags onto the vinyl-
veiled gamma grass; where each night I will sleep, sometimes
too easily, my pillow smoothing over the rocks beneath my back.

I Kept Thinking Back

a collaboration with Alayna Eagle Shield, featuring quotes from her great-great grandmother, Moving Robe Woman

I

August 11th—that first day of construction

It felt just helpless—watching
trucks dump dirt in the ditch.

People stood in the road waving
flags and beating drums, singing prayer songs
or the AIM song. I thought, dangitt,

the tribe didn't agree. They never
got that impact report. We never
surrendered this land. No matter
how many times or how many ways we said no

still they came.

Cops stood like flies around the orange fence.

I heard a man say you might as well stab me
in the heart now, you're going to poison our water.

I am going to tell you of the greatest battle.

I kept hearing the stories of our people.

II

Oh my God the next day I remember waking up crying.
I knew something was going to happen.

We got to the highway early. I just remember
how everything smelled like earth
turned over.

The day was hot and sultry.

I thought of my ancestors
hunting or digging timsila or picking wild grapes
here—

Several of us girls were digging wild turnips.

These Dine ladies said, we were scouting all night,
the police are close, on Highway 6.
Someone said cover your face with a rag
but we were just there to pray. We were only praying when

I was several miles from Hunkpapa camp when

the cop cars came over the hill in this military line-up

I was like holy shit holy shit

beyond a ridge of bluffs in the east

I knew then what my ancestors saw

a cloud of dust began to rise.

III

They came over the hill, crossed
Backwater Bridge, pulling into dying
grass or the middle of the road.

We saw soldiers on horseback across the Greasy Grass River.

Everyone was asking—
what are you going to do?
Will you leave or get arrested?

I dropped the pointed ash stick I used for digging
and ran toward my thípi.

Chus!—I said—what about my future?
What if I'm stuck in jail? What about

My mother told me the news my brother had been killed.

my kids? Then the cops walked out in formation

The soldiers were forming a battle line.

almost perfectly along the dotted line
we heard on the megaphone

I heard a volley of carbines.

you have five minutes
to finish your prayers and leave.

IV

The cops counted down.   4 minutes.

One of the men said, this is the land
of the buffalo people, when buffalo are in danger

We saw a warrior shouting

women and children gather
and the men face out and surround them.

that women and children should run for the hills

I kept thinking back to how scared our people were.

The soldiers began firing into our camp.
The bullets shattered the thípi poles.

I was thinking of the future—when my kids
tell this story. How could I be a good relative?
A good mom?

How could I fight for them?

I sang a death song for my
brother. My heart was bad.

2 minutes.

Everyone walked away. Everyone
cleared the area. And I couldn't
even think anymore.

I was alone at first. They kept announcing
"You'll be arrested. You'll be

The death songs made me brave.

arrested. I was shaking. I turned back

I painted my face with crimson

to the land, wrapped my arms through the bars

braided my black hair.

of the cattle grate. I was shaking. They grabbed

I was
mourning.

for my ear. I stayed. I tried to lili. It felt like

I was a woman but I was not
afraid.

I didn't have a choice.

I didn't have a choice.

Postcard from Standing Rock

I wish you were here.
I know, every day
I was supposed to leave
yesterday. Pack up
the hollow bones of the tent,
stop feeling, each night, like a stowaway
in the sway of the grass.
But,
you
know how I love
this work, the tiny snapping turtles in the river,
the wild plums, tart on my tongue,
my days full with kids weaving drums, the bright sinew
holding everything together.

You're already back in Missouri, keeping lit our garage-sale lamps,
when, after school, Val and Alayna surprise me
with the camper, *home, sweet home* sign hung on the door,
and the deep blue curtains Val stitched just for me,
with strawberry pop-tarts in the cabinets,
nestling in like honeysuckle nectar.

And I know then, I can stay. And I will,

nestling in like honeysuckle nectar:
with strawberry pop-tarts in the cabinets,
and the deep blue curtains Val stitched just for me,
With the camper, *home, sweet home* sign hung on the door.

When after school, Val and Alayna surprised me,
you were already back in Missouri, keeping lit our garage-sale lamps,
holding everything together.

My days full with kids weaving drums, bright sinew;
the wild plums, tart on my tongue;
this work; the tiny snapping turtles in the river.
Know how I love
you. But
in the sway of the grass,
I stop feeling, each night, like a stowaway.
The hollow bones of the tent
packed up yesterday.
I was supposed to leave,
I know. Every day,
I wish you were here.

ARRESTS TO DATE: 60

We Don't Know Yet That the Little Girl is Safe

Our flashlights weave a trembling

net across the prairie, sway for hours like river grass

underwater. She's four; rumor says, last seen

with two white men. We pass this panicked offering

to one another like sharp crusts of stale bread.

Sometimes, in the dark of a slope, our lights catch

the ghosts of other missing girls, from each nation

whose flag flies above our hand-built home.

They're lacing a child's shoe, or a needle and thread,

finishing a poem, or a tattoo, an argument,

or a college class; busy with everything

uncompleted, the women who have not

been found. We yell her name again, again, again, each syllable

pleating in our mouths like a luminescent shell. The echo

catches in each thípi flap, clutches at each blade

of grass. We snake our small lights between the ribs

of horse trailers, through every ash and cottonwood

copse. Every bed is left empty and rumpled, every

sleeping bag, splayed. Some of us begin to unzip

each tent; and by the bank of the river, some kneel,

shining what beam they can toward the bottom.

Rally at the Capital

Bismark, ND

Camp bursts from busses, vans, opens like an agate
 on the state-sponsored lawn. Uniform
and over-mowed blades obscured now by the flash

of jingle dresses, jewel-toned *I Stand with Standing Rock*
 tees. *Water is Life* signs float like sails,
let us believe our collective bodies could be

a boat. Ricardo shares a sketch, a small girl
 placing a flower in the gaping throat
of a gun; the ends of Red Fawn's ribbon skirt

flutter like the cobalt butterflies back at camp;
 and everyone chants *Protect the Sacred, Protect
the Sacred.* We round dance, rise and fall like one

set of lungs. Our skyward fists are a release
 of balloons. And none of this requires
the rows of National Guard men swaddled

in riot gear, matched and ill-fitting pants.
 I lay on the grass beside a huddle
of quiet kids. RJ asks why there are so many

cops, so many guns, when nobody has done
 anything violent? Halle says, *they want us
to start getting afraid.* The monolith

of men shadow us like the brutalist
    building they line up before.
The obligatory blankness in their faces

blurring and disappearing the bowed
    lips, birthmarks, moles, the small
asymmetries their lovers must think of at night.

FLOODPLAIN

No matter how scary things got, every morning, we would pray by the river. Someone would light the sage and I'd think about all the things I'm thankful for, like how we're by the river and we have clean water and we had breakfast and the sun is coming up. I'd start praying for the water and people who were sick or were troubled at that time. We'd always put our hands in the river. It was so cool and I could feel it between my fingers as it was flowing down the stream. I'd feel more with myself. More like myself.

FRANKIE ARCHAMBAULT

age 15 (age 11 at camp)

A Lesson in Word Choice

Our army tent turned school
rattles with exhaust
from the helicopters, shakes
with shards of speeches from the Sacred Fire.

dog bite.   breast.   bulldozer.   burial sites.

The big kids and I brace
our heads on our fists, circle like petals
on the dirt damp rug, the Bismarck Tribune
the pistil in the middle.

Jayden begins the headline:

<u>Protestors</u>

They call us protestors, he says, *to make it sound*
like we want to fight, but we're protectors.
We protect the water
for everyone.

Yesterday started as a prayer walk:
banners   regalia   cedar   children   chatting   chanting
pouring luminous as a river into the container
of the highway's edge

until somebody got a call: bulldozers carving
the pipeline path, like something opposite a birth,
through the fields west of Highway 1806.

The words *voluntary suspension of construction* broken,
on sacred spaces
the tribe had filed, yesterday, to protect.

Injure

We arrived to land like a pale
welt, raw and exposed.
Prairie crocus, deep-rooted echinacea,
and the burial places,
churned unrecognizable.
Behind barbed wire, the growl
of bulldozers, glossy
German Shepard tongues.

Dogs

Frankie says,
they don't even say the dogs were biting people,
It's like we *attacked* them *first.*

In the chaos of rising fists, horses painted with hands,
ticking helicopter blades, canine noses
wet with blood:

it was the women,
grasping one another, who lay down
where the mouth of the dozer was meant to swallow
next, planted

their bodies until the machine retreated.
I watched like a scarecrow, strung outside
the fence by my own indecision
as their ribbon skirts re-colored the land.

Tashubi kicks a box,
sloppy with summer tank tops, half-used
grammar books donated
from white people's basements,

at Construction Site

It's not just a place to dig up—it's our land!
Our ancestors are buried here. The treaties say it's ours!

I hear the little kids ask José about tear gas
again, their arms waving and purple with glitter,
if the cops will spray kids too.

And I know some things
I didn't know last week. How I should have
poured milk on the welted face
of the blue-haired woman
on the side of the road.
How I can waver
like a building
glimpsed through heat when it's my turn
to put my body on the line
and how that is a violence too.

Through the speaker, we hear a fragment
of an elder's speech: a reminder
that every choice we make is a ceremony.

Our faces are green in the tent's military-issue glow,
                    and a few miles away, in St. Anthony,
          red and blue lights of police
barb a fence around each school bus,
                              escort white children back
                                        to white homes,
                    and when the state says *protect,*
we all know who they mean.

Očhéthi, the day after the clearing of Treaty Camp

We've been told *hundreds of arrests.*
Held in dog kennels. Strip searched.
Told even grandmas, praying
and smoke-haloed from inípi, were thrown
to the ground. Told the pipeline
will cross the road to Cannonball Ranch,
touch the untouched sacred sites
by Wednesday. We've been told
that we lost. Still, the kids

need breakfast. Somehow, the sun rises
over the walk from closed cookshack
to closed cookshack, sky swollen as a bruised
plum, purpling the smoke of the thípis.
In the distance, two women kneel
on the plywood roof of a half-built
house, bodies clad in the fawn-colored
fabric of their Carhartt jumpers, ladders
pawing behind them like restless
cats. They staple a vinyl tarp
to the slight slope. Here's

a list of everything I know: I will find
breakfast. They will cover
the roof. When I walk by the house
again, it will look like a woman, braced
against the October wind, the tarp
a skirt she smooths against her hips.

ARRESTS TO DATE: 411

Woman Charged with Attempted Murder of Law Enforcement Officer

Date: October 31, 2016

Agency: Morton County

Mandan, N.D. - The Morton County States Attorney's office charged 37 year-old Red Fawn Fallis

who called me Chitty Chatty Bang Bang, as I trailed her camp to camp,
who marched a waving rainbow of ribbon skirt through still-tall grass,

with attempted murder (class A felony), preventing arrest (C felony), carrying a concealed weapon,

a bag of flat leaf cedar, for ceremony, in the band of her skirt. She held the resined
needles between us, and they branched like capillaries, which is to say, like prayer.

(A misdemeanor), possession of marijuana (B misdemeanor), criminal conspiracy to commit endangering by fire

she offered tobacco, asked elders what they could teach
Beadwork, they said, hand drums, stories of Iktómi
and the ducks' red eyes. She wrote answers
in her pencil's soft lead.

(C felony), maintaining a public nuisance (A misdemeanor) and engaging in a riot (B misdemeanor).

In September, before the oil money spotlights,

we were guided only
by pollen-scattered
stars.

And Red Fawn,

though the plains grew thigh-high and we worried for snakes,

you led us, your strong boots bending the stems to bring us
home.

We end up at a buffalo butchering after the Halloween party

Two men struggle, pull at the hide where its belly is slit like a seam, constellate
the thick fur with their headlamps, small beside the crude oil spotlights that bleach
the sky of stars now. A woman with a purple bandana slices the membrane,
exposed, thin as moon. The animal pops apart, knob-kneed, leg flung
toward the kids shivering in my lap. RJ whispers "pilamaya'ye tȟatȟáŋka
for the stew and the taco meat." We nod, polyester ninja suits and tiger tails
dampening in the grass, snicker wrappers circling us like rocks around a fire.
Three days since Treaty Camp was raided, since I drove them in circles
all night past dark thípis and empty trailers, past ambulances clustered
like a scab by the waving flag road. All of us eating trunk-stale oreos
and dry ramen, crooning too loud to some song nobody liked.
Everyone knew better than to ask for their family. I'm a zombie still.
Or half of one anyway, in dollar store make-up done up by the girls.
Shawnee Rae holds my face in her hands, delicate as if I'm a bundle
of bird bones, dabs baby wipes at the green sludge beneath my eyes, the blood
on my mouth. The buffalo's fat-frosted muscle glistens now, runs in streams,
the animal red and hideless in the too-bright night. "We look like that inside,"
Shawnee pauses to say. RJ says "In the old days, they killed them with bows,
but now they use guns." Shaylena shakes her head, "No, only cops have those."

Standing Rock Nocturne

for Noah

Tonight, our books, our blender, our bed, these small talismans
of domesticity, and you, feel far from the sigh of the patched

camper window, its lung of ziploc and electrical tape rasping
out the rhythm of the drums, the lilis and akishas; far from these stippled

curtains that feel, sometimes, like the whole universe; far from the pipeline
pictures the kids taped to the cabinets' veneer. I wish I had hiked the frozen hill

tonight for reception, called to tell you, *forgive me for not calling sooner.*
No, I wish I had braved the snow to say, *every day is more*

difficult and beautiful than I could have imagined. No.
I know, what I should have told you: *I can be far from you*

because of you. I should have thanked you for the place you hold,
tangled (I imagine) in our cheap sheets, our ketubah still balancing

on its single nail above your head. Thank you, because I know I can return,
crawl to you, asleep in our bed, and you'll murmur, shore me to the steady

beat of the blood in your chest. How I'll whisper about the one wasp
who lived with me here through all of October. How gently it rested,

nights on my cheek, how we would both have faith we could stay
still like this: learn not to hurt one another. Thank you for tending

our houseplants in my absence, even the Christmas Cactus
we thought was dead, for your unflagging belief in the bright

bloom that comes suddenly during seasons of snow, and for your hands
keeping each small thing alive, turning each pot toward the sun.

There are No Police in this Poem

Only the kids/balancing in their snow boots/
the log beneath them/rainbowed in resistance
slogans/slushgrey light/interrupted by the bright
flags/of their arms/they wave down our
car/"teachers! teachers!"/we unclick/the loose
tooth/of each manual lock/and the dinged up
doors/full weight of the kids/on their
handles/fly open/ like the arms of startled
infants/*there are no police in this poem/*   o n l y
Shawnee Rae/   my foot as her
springboard/vaulting to the console/asterisking
my borrowed skirt/with the juice/of her gas-
station pickle/only Shelby's hands/winging
/my books from the backseat/ and
Shaylena/who can't be bothered/   wedging
her knees/   into the narrow volumes
of poetry/slick picture book covers/ I'm saying/
there are no police in this/   car
/where Frankie lunges over/   everybody/
her arms/and long black cape of a coat/wrapped
around Baby Dylan/   marshmallow-manned
in his snowsuit/   fingers sour-patch sticky/
somehow/   suddenly/my hands/   my feet/
are off/   the wheel/   the pedals/   I am/
ankle-deep in the snow/all the teachers are/
shivering spectators of this/   wild joy/ and
I can see/   it doesn't belong to me/   but
I can love it anyhow/*there are no police/*
anywhere/   as Emma's elbow/   pokes
the horn/beep beeeep beeeeeeeep/ jostling
through the snow/   muffle of prairie/

as Reina and Nyla and RJ/ co-sardine the driver's
seat/ getaway curls/smooshed on the
felt/ of the ceiling/ *there are no/*
seats left in the car/ so Michael and Layton/
scramble the windshield/ sprawl
on the roof/ *there are/*
only the kids/ shouting the ecstatic
tally of themselves/ one two three/
all the way to fourteen/ as they
take this frame/ that looked so
inflexible/ and/*there/*
make space for each of
their bodies.

Prairie Knights Casino

It's true. Some nights I leave

the disarray of donations, frost-lipped boxes spilling
uselessly into the dark; the woodstove, always begging us

to chap our hands on the hatchet
in the wind-raw night and—
I drive and drive
to the fluorescence of Prairie Knights, promised land

of internet and limp quesadillas. Here, camp blossoms
into the buffet line and business center; our phones find every

outlet and our hat-smashed hair oils
the vinyl chairs beneath the bustle

display and in the pool's chlorinated hall. Everybody shares
the latest gossip: who's running the cookshack,
the oncoming snow, the day's arrests.

But I find myself hiding in the windowless orange light
of the Schwan's machine room; alone
to lean the spasms in my back against the glow

of the beef stroganoff button. For the first time in a week, I take off
my coat. I've come with notebooks to grade, funds to raise for bales
to keep us from the cold; but instead I scroll and I scroll: stare at blooms

of lavender lattes, friends on hikes, at bars, cooking dinner, arms
posed around their husbands and I never
say anything to them.

Maybe I'll cocoon in the casino forever, dragging soggy fries through an eternal
river of ketchup or I'll drive the fourteen hours to a city where I own

a bed. But even as the empty vein
of the pipeline pushes further and further, as storm-bent
tents sing the songs of hollow shells, and my spine

forgets how to hold me: I'll drive north

past the pastured horses, ice glittering on their eyelashes, the cars
blizzarded into the ditch. Head north toward the gate
where someone will shine a beam in my car, say go on in, welcome home.

These leavings a privilege I want and don't want. The night a salt shaker of stars.

On Building a School

Shaylena, age 9, of Hot Pink Coat and Perfect Scrambled Eggs,
presses her velcroed boot against the wire
of ice and barbs, opens the fence that keeps us
from the river.

She tells me what she heard about the Sacred Objects,
returned by the county after the raid,
hand-fringed hide of the čhaŋnúŋpa bags,
deer-given skin of the drums,
stained yellow with the piss of police.

I crawl through the passage,
past the cottonwood choking
with leafless vine, the abandoned
nest of the snow bunting,
preserved in its sheath of ice.
She speaks of these handmade objects

and I think of what we are trying
to build, this idea we call a school.
I think of a friend who said:
Native tradition creates beauty
in every object- a reminder
to care for what you have.

I've spent years with the disposable
test booklets, the tiny eyes
of each multiple choice, classrooms with four
reliable walls. Years believing
I could know what was best.

Shaylena of Six Sisters, of Telling Adults
to Stop Screaming about Cops
and Scaring the Kids,
leads me down a sandy slope,
away from the road that spins
with pick-up trucks packed with lumber, ladders, tent poles:
these fragments that will re-build
the homes that were taken last week,
re-build homes we all know
may be taken again.
We dip to a slim cuticle of a bank, frozen,
freckled today with trash.
Months ago, the kids built
a ramshackle bridge here, the driftwood glittering
jade with algae, the splintering damp
in the sun. They climbed to the edge, unbothered
that the bridge reached no certain bank,
scrambled on scraped hands and knees
and trusted the rotting of the wood,
or maybe trusted, even, the fall.

The first time somebody mentioned staying the winter,
among the horse games and giveaways of August,
I laughed— the story of my skin made me
believe we'd win history
quickly, go home. How will I know how
to name this, for the kids,
for myself, if we fail?

Shaylena digs in the cold sand,
unearths a skittles wrapper,
the rainbow mud-fossiled into brittle bird.
I am about to warn her to stay away
from the water's cold edge, when she slips the trash
gently into my hand, says *šá*,
next, hands me a crinkled lay's bag, *zí*,
a ramen wrapper, *šázi* .

She hands me each Lakȟóta color,
picks up each piece
one-by-one, as if we'd never heard
the ambulances screech
from the road, as if the helicopters
didn't scar the air
with their mosquito song.
She names each item as if
there was no other sound in the world
for what we held in our hands.

Thanksgiving

Green pop-up tents bloom,
patchouli-scented, from swampy patches
of melted snow. The paths we used to take
fill with the stakes
of people playing hacky sack. Fill with their wood-eating
bonfires and acoustic guitars. In the biodome,
extra breath condenses to sharp
sheets of ice, dangles above our heads.
Every day is a whitening road, Johnnie quips
in morning meeting and I overhear a woman,
blonde hair spilling from her knitted cap,
call herself Sičháŋǧu, because of where she's placed her tent.
The new people are checking in
on facebook, skirting between the men and women
chopping wood to take
pictures of themselves
beside the thípis. One man tells me
he's come to run the school
and will be leaving on Tuesday. Even the porta-potties are totally
full of shit, forcing everyone's ass to cautiously hover the rim.
I like to think I belong here
despite my skin, that I can remember
my own limitations. But still, to the kids, I chirp
are you happy so many people are here
to support you?
Michael shrugs—
do they know their tents
are in my basketball court?

(On the Phone, You Say "I Don't Know If I Can Do This Anymore")

at the bottom   of the hill where I'm parked
                                        the only hill

            where I can reach you

a camper. windows filling   with fire.

      heat charring an orchid

                  around each pane
of exploded fiberglass.

Smoke tendrils my car &

                  the empty solar charging station &

      the ice-crisped legal tent,

                  cracks in the frozen air.

People gather at the flame
                  like a backward video
            of snow   scattering the road.

(I have to go. I have to go. I say. I'm needed here.)

I abandon
the car

the snapped joint of the visor
muffler held on by phone cords

try to leave everything

broken there & run again

but I've gone where I'm not needed. the camper is a petrified shell:

someone's favorite slippers, cereal boxes,
that one good blanket,
already turned to wick,
then soft ash.

A man I don't know hugs me
holds my wet face to his chest. It's okay, it's okay.

I try to say that's not mine.

From here, I see

the Pontiac is almost beautiful

in its rosettes of snow, like a statue

I understand, the man says, I've lost a home too.

firm on the frosting of a cake.

Exposure (Two Police Statements Six Days Apart)

I am confident

winter temperatures can be deceiving

the decision made to use water

prolonged exposure to cold air

was the correct one

can be deadly

said Sheriff Kyle Kirchmeier.

Pantoum (Obstructed) with Army Corps Decision & Lice Treatment on Abandoned Bus

O how we itch but how we glisten! Look, the medics run warm tea tree hands through our hair and
here, the kids wear emergency blankets like capes. They jump and this whole bus silvers, torn seats singing
with superhero spells. Never mind that there is no room left in the medic yurt to treat our small bodies
in warmth. Never mind the stories of the state. I have said it again and again, please see this joy

here: the kids clutching emergency blankets like capes. Even as the whole bus shivers, our skin stinging
with wind snaked through half-cracked glass. Even as the balm on our scalps congeals and loses
its warmth. Never mind the stories of the state. I have said it again and again, please see this joy
falling apart each day in our fingers. The desicison is clear: ETP can't brand the water with pipes

that snake like wind through half-cracked glass. Still, I know the balm on our scalps will congeal and lose
to these bugs, fattened on the blood of the kids, who crack hand warmers so hard black dust bleeds out,
falls apart in our fingers. ETP is clear: they'll ignore the decision, brand the water with pipes
like they have the land beside the river. Oil eddies on our skin and I can't find a way to believe anymore

they won't fatten on the blood of the earth, crack it so hard black dust bleeds out
like a greedy spell, never mind how they state

(The state says)

there is no room anywhere for all our small bodies

(they'll send us away)

especially beside the river.
Oil eddies

(insists this place isn't safe)

everywhere we feel our skin.
I can't find a way anymore to believe

(for the kids)

how we glistened.

(but where have they left)

Each night now,

(untouched?)

we feel cold hands in our hair.

December

The turtles press like brown gems
into the Cannonball's ring of river mud, shush
the speed of their hearts. Beneath the ice, their bodies
remember this slow waltz of survival.

In the yurt, we're low on wood. For days
the kitchen serves
half-frozen soup.

The black-capped chickadees,
light as a palm of paperclips, stay
alive by sinking their temperature like a stone,
choosing to let hypothermia
through the doors of their feathers,
the vaulted windows of their bones.

Rivulets snake from the treads
of our boots:
dampen our sleeping bags,
freeze in our socks.

In the gravel light of the storm,
raccoons grapple their fingers, bury their masks
in the warm musk of one another, their hollowed
tree filling with heat.

Our gloves drip from the blue-
tarped ceiling, its wooden poles, a sky raining
with empty hands.
The writers of history call this
civilization: how far we are from the ways
we've kept our own bodies warm.

CONFLUENCE

At camp it was like, we were all a family. There were so many people but it felt small because you could walk everywhere and you knew everybody and everything. When it ended, it was like our home got taken.

SHAYLENA BLACK ELK

age 13 (age 9 at camp)

By the Numbers

Date: March 16, 2017
Agency: North Dakota Joint Information Center

BISMARCK, ND – The North Dakota Highway Patrol logged more hours in flight during the six months of the Dakota Access Pipeline protest than they would typically fly over the course of four years.[1]

DAPL-related NDHP Aircraft Hours	612
Number of Flights	241
Average Time per Flight	2.5

[1] The white noise of the helicopters still brushes my skin like a nightgown, leaves red welts in the shape of eyes. I wake with my keys in my hands, ready, if they come, to take the students and run.

January, After Camp

Listen. I don't want to keep touching the interior
of my house, want to stop
leaning in the stairwell, tapping each exposed
brick, one by one
mortar coating my fingers like lunar dust.
I want to want to stop running

my finger along the edge
of the formica table, flipping the lights
on and off and on and off and off.
No, I don't want to talk about it.

But, could you give me
a word for the opposite
of a miracle? What if the fish stopped dividing
before everyone was fed?
Or the Red Sea contracted
on the final stragglers?
What do we say now that the camp is disappearing
and the pipeline isn't? What do I call this

warm bed and phone signal,
this house, where I'm not needed
to chop wood or find breakfast,
to walk with the kids along the river?

The doctors say I'm here until spring
my herniated spine
a boat that's left me on this shore.
Back at camp, they're disassembling

the yurt, pulling down each pole
that held our small sky,
packing the never-finished
books the kids were writing
into whatever boxes they can find.

What if I don't see any options besides being there
or pretending it never happened?

A magazine tells me, on Mt. Sinai
scientists have discovered a way to read a palimpsest,
written-over stories still legible in their depressions.
They tell me, what's beautiful
or terrible
can never be erased
and I close the pages,

let the battery drain
on my phone, open the amber
bottles of pills that sometimes
let me forget
the pain long enough to sit
in a chair a minute or two, walk unassisted
to the kitchen, the bathroom.

I wear my boots to watch tv.
white-knuckled, clutching a throw pillow
like a steering wheel. I'm home.
My husband tells me to take off my coat.

By the Numbers

Date: March 16, 2017

Agency: North Dakota Joint Information Center

BISMARCK, ND – The following numbers are a breakdown of the vehicles abandoned and towed from the Očhéthi camp.

Total Vehicles Abandoned	**44**
Trucks/Pick-ups	13
Vans	2
Cars	12
Snow Blade/Removal	1
Snowmobile Sleds	4
Flatbed Trailers	6
Campers/Motorhomes	3[2]
Log Splitter	1
Buses	2

[2] I'm lucky. Mine isn't one of them. Dragged by Val to the casino just ahead of the bulldozer tracks. In the months I spend in bed, I try each day to forget it. Not to imagine it there, in the farthest corner of the parking lot, drifts heaped against the aluminum like dirty laundry. Cabinets swung open, exposing particle board hearts. Socks toppled into the sink, iced into inhuman shapes. The ziploc-covered window must be torn to flimsy teeth, snow swelling the pictures the kids drew, their journals, my lessons. Soaking the Star Quilt, mildewing the sunset-colored piecework. We all thought we could come back for what we left.

Baking Bread as Očhéthi Šakówiŋ is Raided

I.

Nobody stands at North Gate anymore,
when bulldozers lumber the slope, score
the dirt with their teeth, scatter
men who slash thípis in the wet earth
where we once lived.

Winona's kitchen,
the tent where the kids donned rubber gloves
ladled soup into hundreds of bowls,
crumples like a foal in the snow.

The sheriff calls this *victory*
I am very happy to say that we finally introduced
rule of law in the Očhéthi camp,

and I am not there.
I don't want to tell you this,
but I am leaning against my stove
in St. Louis, clutching a recipe's flimsy page,
written in black and white, as the blurry window of my
computer
streams Očhéthi in from the edge of my counter.
I am just a woman whose back will not support her,
in a city that hides its water
behind high voltage lines and highway,
starburst windows of forgotten factories.

The bulldozers power
toward the Cannonball, river I slept beside,
churn the earth and the roots
of each plant as central heat pumps
like an old heart through my house.

2.

I used to trust in the words
that were placed on my tongue.
I called the river *Missouri*
but learned no language
for the dams, redirecting the water,
holding back the stories
of the silt and the clay.
I never learned of the children
who were taken from its side. I never learned why
I was taught to sing
"This land is my land."

3.

The county commissioner says,
he's *proud* the camp was cleared
without any major injuries
and I remove a glass measuring cup from my shelf.
Travis's plywood home, where he practiced
the songs he would sing with the kids,
the home he built with his hands, spray-painted,
"We are unarmed," erupts into flames.

I unfold the origami of the flour's
silent mouth. The bulldozers turn and shred
haybales that kept our thípis warm in the wind, yank
the foundation from Tonia's wigwam,
where Shaylena and Shawnee
last hugged me goodbye. The bag coughs
flour like dandelion seed, and I cannot
come clean of it: coating my fingers white, wedged
white between the threads of my sweater,
burrowed white
in the split wood of my counter.

On the screen, assault rifles
push the last few people to the river.

4.

Some days, I lean against my sink,
feel the grinding in my spine and I am ashamed
to say, that some small piece of me wishes I could close
this window, simply follow the directions,
that have been written so clearly before me,
let my world be the chipped white of my cabinets
the shift of the pots and pans above my head,
forget I ever lived beside a river.

But the Missouri and the Mississippi
become one and reach me, even here,
each time I turn my tap.

When the edges of the Cannonball overflow,
touch the places along the riverbank
where we sought sticks for drums,
and studied the plants and sat in circles and sang,
the water runs here.
Everyday, I brush my teeth with Očhéthi,
Everyday, I wash my clothes with Očhéthi.
Everyday, it is Očhéthi that fills my glass.

5.

On the feed, the soldiers are chasing Eric
who made tea for our coughs,
dipping into jars of marshmallow root
and ginger and osha. Once he measured herbs
with the kids, as I measure my water
to the line, stir until strands of gluten begin to form.
The camera bucks and I see only a river of sky
and Eric is screaming.

6.

The governor says he is glad
the efforts have gone so *smoothly*
and, one-by-one each feed blinks out.

7.

What we built is now just mud and sleet,
ash and firewood, broken
by bulldozer chains. Still, I see

the Sacred Fire in the summer, Frankie
braiding my hair in the food line,
Wolf and Junior grass dancing
in the firelight. I don't know

when the pipeline will run
beneath the river, when the water will brush
its strange plastic tubes before it reaches our lips.
I don't know if this bread will ever rise or
when or where

the first oil will leak.
But I am learning something small of how
to see a river: to see the drowning hidden
beneath the water, and see also, the kids on the bank
covered in temporary tattoos, hair spiked from days
of swimming. They are praying
for the construction workers
Help them understand, their kids drink water too.
Tobacco sprinkles from their fingers,
is taken in the breath of the current.

In the Hospital, I Wake, Still Believing I Belong to Everything

My body is Highway 1806, snakeskin
        secreted in river grass, and the pitchy chirp
of the machine beside my ear, making linear
        the story of my pulse, and the meadowlark's
crushed tail feathers, still ruffled in the wind
        of the semis, and the nurses who check me,
and the flies fucking loudly in the grass, and the soft breath
        of pencils on the chart. My body is the suspended
ceiling, tiles racing in dirty currents above my head,
        and the river-smooth acorn and the crinkled
periwinkle curtain, shushing the room in two.
        Tonight I can't remember the drums'
nightly rhythms and my body is the small jeweled
        cries my roommate sends up from her sleep
and the dress coat balled beneath Noah's head
        as his shoulders twist against the vinyl chair.
My body is a four-inch incision, packaged
        in gauze, and the path of someone else's
scalpel through my spine, and a stranger's hands
        on the small of my back. Tell me, faded blue flowers
of the hospital gown, bag of morphine,
        bag of saline, do you think it's snowing
there tonight? I had to give up a piece of me
        in order to walk again. My body is a body, healing,
in a neurosurgery ward. The lights that bloom
        along my wired arm are only the EKG.

By the Numbers

Date: March 7, 2017

Agency: North Dakota Joint Information Center

BISMARCK, ND – A snapshot of resources and costs diverted from normal operations[3] to support State and Local response to ensure public safety and law and order in Morton County and the Bismarck region due to protest events and related illegal activity since August 10, 2016.

Days of Response Support	210
Hours of Response Support	331,721
State and Local Cost to Taxpayers (estimated as of March 6, 2017)	$38.2M[4]
◦ Personnel (Salaries, EMAC)	$30M
◦ Personnel Support (Travel and per diem, lodging)	$4.1M
◦ Equipment/Supplies (Cold weather gear, radios, gas)	$4.1M
In State Agencies Providing Support	106
Other States Providing Support	10
Out of State Agencies Providing Support	34[5]

[3] Each sleeping bag held somebody who had given something up. Something bartered for those days spent chopping firewood, marching the shoulder of 1806, sorting cans of beans, snow-soaked labels peeling off in their hands. Each person, curled at night like a vine, learning to sleep still in the shadows of the body's own warmth, had bartered something to see, for once, the river win.

[4] The US Department of Justice "awarded" $10 million dollars to the state of North Dakota for their "efforts" during the NoDapl movement. Energy Transfer Partners donated the following: $15 million to the State of North Dakota, $5 million to the University of Mary, $35,000 to North Dakota 4-H, $35,000 to North Dakota FFA, $140,000 to North Dakota Emergency Management Services along the pipeline route, $20,000 to Ipswich County, $20,000 to Campbell County, $20,000 to McPherson County, $20,000 to Beadle County, $20,000 to…

[5] On the coldest nights, you could hear these other lives. Broken housing contracts and paystubs-that-never-were fluttering their wings in the wind. The sleeves of the cheap jackets piling up in donations, somehow lifted into moonlight by the arms of family members left behind. Heirloom jewelry, bartered for gas money, clicking its clasps beneath the heartbeat of the drums. Jobs, pets, time, cash, houses. Gone. Floated up like the hovering smoke of thípis in December. Then, the burial sites west of the road. Gone. The easement keeping the pipeline from the river. Gone. Sacred Spaces east of the road. Gone. And then, the camp was too.

Spring

1.

The magnolias, that looked for months skeletal
as wind-blown tents, turn waxy and raw and pink
with blossom. This is supposed to hurt—
my neurosurgeon says about the thin needles
embroidering my every step, my nerves fumbling
to relearn their pathways, their firings,
the small machinery that makes me feel.

2.

Alayna and Val send the Star Quilt,
snowmelt between its seams writing
the history of these lost months in mold.
Orange and brown diamonds I traced each night
with my gloves, hidden beneath dirt
like webbing on a mountain, or the layer of rainbow
oil on a puddle.

The kids and I begin
to find ways to find one another.
They sleep now in their home
or somebody's sofa   or a car
or another camp. I text Frankie—
what was the most important thing about Očhéthi?
she says—we weren't afraid to stand up
for what we love.

3.

My doctor mandates ten-minute walks,
and the rain-glittered sidewalks are Pollocks
of worms, sliding in and out of themselves.

  Somehow, this collapse moves them
to the next square of concrete. Teresa, you were wrong
            to believe you'd be able
                                        to never feel again
wrong to believe   you would never let yourself
            see anything as beautiful anymore.
Your husband cleans the quilt.
Let him touch your back,
            dress the wound. It's okay
if you can still see the seam.

ARRESTS TO DATE: 761

Confluence

Here, at this half-ass state park without a sign,
        with its cracked concrete bench and triangle of dying
cottonwoods, the Missouri joins the Mississippi,
        meeting not like a ballet, or a twisting
of silk scarves, but maybe like construction workers, shaking
        hands before a building forever half-built.
And what is there to do now but love this unfinished work
        of the river, carrying everything it has ever been
given: snow-melt streams like a cold bandana circling
        its neck, shreds of styrofoam cooler catching
in its teeth, sturgeon eggs blooming with their translucent
        tails, nitrates, and phosphates, and soil glittering
with bone, and this single mountain dew bottle
        eddying in a green-tinged foam, and the ashes
of Očhéthi, reddening in all of our throats. I sit with my knees
        tucked to my chest, listen to the ducks call
each other from either side of what will be
        the same water, and River, you and I both know
that despite your dams, you will go on
        to grow deadly algae in the Gulf, to feed rich
alluvial plains, shelter alligators and hellbenders and mudpuppies,
        to have done to you and to do the most beautiful
and terrible things. We know the word end
        is never an end, but always a mouth instead.

* * *

An Invitation to an Eclipse Party

I am wearing a dress of fist-sized
polka dots and, for you, friend, serving moon
pies and lunar-colored cheeses.
It might as well be a wedding,
I am so in love with each person
collapsed on the comforter
of faded ducks or playing fetch
with the dogs from discount camp chairs, arms
outstretched and ready with a rubber ball.

Look, beneath the oak,
my husband feathers
with a million crescent suns, turning
his hair to foreign thicket, scattering
the hands I know best
by their touch on my stomach.
We are trying to have a child. You
are the first one I've told.

You know all this:
how there's no more cookshack at Očhéthi,
no more corn drying beneath red tarps,
giant pots to scrub,
or help-yourself mint and echinacea tea,
How the school is just the mildewed skin of a yurt
and I understand something now
of how a whole world can disappear—
and you know too, how last week, white supremacists rioted in Charlottesville,
how we saw their militia; Hitler t-shirts, sharp
scythes of swastika flags.

How they called in their chants for the man I love
and our child, small unexistant planet,
bit of uncongregated light,
to burn in the dark, disappear
beneath their hands. And how

could I invite anyone here,
where blades of grass silver before us
and cicadas sound their alarms,
when I know I cannot protect them?

But, as the pugs run orbits
around their own
surreal shadows and the gnats panic
from the butterfly bush,
as we lose piece after piece
of sun, let me give you these small
cardboard glasses. Let's share the sweetness
of the remaining oreos, take bright
swings of half-drunk sunny delight.

I believed once some myths
about this day and others,
most recently that all light could be
lost, the center could go dark
entirely. But astronomers say, even in totality,
when our eyes detect only
a hungry hole of sky,
the moon is glowing (faint, but no matter),
with earthshine. So enamored am I
of our strange starlight, reflected
and refracted again and again, but still there;
everything the shadows cannot extinguish.

Notes

Many of the kids from the school at camp are in the process of writing their own poems about Mní Wičhóni Nakíčižiŋ Owáyawa. These quotes come from our first brainstorming conversations and are used, of course, with their permission.

"The Naming of Facebook Hill": The cartoonist in this poem is Kewa artist Ricardo Caté. You can find more of his work, including his cartoons about camp here: https://www.facebook.com/WithoutReservations.

"Learning the Plum Pit Game": Pilamaya'ye (pilamz! pilamz!) to Leksi Steve Tamayo, artist, historian, and expert in Lakȟóta culture for sharing so much of his knowledge, including cunwiyawa, the plum pit game, with our school. You can find more of his artwork here: https://www.facebook.com/Bluebirdartandregalia.

"I Kept Looking Back": My constant appreciation and awe for my sister, Alayna Eagle Shield. The text in this poem comes from conversations between Alayna and me and an interview with her great-great-grandmother, Moving Robe Woman regarding the Battle of Greasy Grass, or Little Bighorn. The interview can be found in "Lakota Recollections of the Custer Fight" (a book whose editorial voice I cannot endorse). This is not a persona poem, but truly a collaboration, crafted together.

"The story starts like this: with scraps of shell": The damming here refers to the Pick-Sloan Project, in which twelve dams were built along the Missouri between 1946-1966 (with seven more dams added between 1976-1994). These dams flooded over 200,000 acres of land on Standing Rock and Cheyenne River reservations alone. Nearly 1,000 Native families were displaced by the dams. Much of Standing Rock's fertile land was lost, destroying traditional culture and food systems along with it. Vine Deloria, Jr. descibed the dams as, "without doubt, the single most destructive act ever perpetrated on any tribe by the United States."

"We Don't Know Yet the Little Girl is Safe": Thankfully, the young girl in this poem was found safe. The incident was a misunderstanding of the type that happens at any large event. The problem of missing and murdered indigenous women, however, is very real. According to the National Crime and Information Center, in 2016, 125 indigenous women were reported missing in North Dakota alone. The true number is likely much higher. On some reservations, women are ten times as likely to be murdered as the national average. You can learn more at http://www.strongheartshelpline.org and http://www.niwrc.org.

"A Lesson in Word Choice": When Tashubi says "the treaties say its ours," she's referring to the fact that the land and water that the pipeline ultimately went through were named as part of the Great Sioux Nation in the 1868 Fort Laramie Treaty, an agreement between two soveriegn nations. However, when the Great Sioux Nation was carved into six different reservations, those spaces became Army Corps of Engineers land, despite having never been ceded. So, while the pipeline pathway crossed near, but not through, the Reservation, according to the treaties (which are legally considered the "law of the land"), it is still Lakȟóta territory.

After this particular lesson, the students decided they wanted to create documentaries to tell their own stories of the movement and camp. You can find some of their work here: https://vimeo.com/album/4324357. You can also learn more about the actual incident through Democracy Now's coverage: https://www.youtube.com/watch?v=kuZcx2zE04k.

"Women Charged with Attempted Murder": Red Fawn was arrested during the violent police-led raid on Treaty Camp, which was approximately three miles north of Očhéthi Šakówiŋ in the place where the pipeline would cross the road. The Cheyenne River Sioux Tribe invoked eminent domain of this unceded treaty land in order to stop construction. The statement here is the exact police statement, with my obvious additions.

"On Building a School": The quote about Native tradition here comes from the scholarship of Sweeney Windchief.

"Exposure": The words in this poem come directly from two North Dakota Highway Patrol statements: "Protestors erect unlawful structures; should seek appropriate winter shelter" (Nov 18, 2016) and "Sidebar: Use of water as a less-than-lethal tool for riot control" (Nov 22, 2016).

"By the Numbers": Each of these are direct police statements. The footnotes are my only additions.

Acknowledgements

The cover image is a detail from a ribbon skirt created by Val Eagle Shield. Val is a gifted artist and knowledge keeper. I am extremely honored to have these poems appear in the presence of her work.

I am grateful to the editors of the publications in which these poems first appeared:

Academy of American Poets (poets.org) – "Baking Bread as Očhéthi Šakówiŋ is Raided"

Beloit Poetry Review – "Postcard from Standing Rock"

Best New Poets – "We End Up at a Buffalo Butchering After the Halloween Party"

BOAAT – "In the hospital, I wake, still believing I belong to everything"

december – "Invitation to an Eclipse Party"

Georgia Review – "Tonight, I haven't even said the word pipeline," "I kept thinking back," "Spring"

Gingko Prize Ecopoetry Anthology – "If you're married, why do you call her Teresa?," "Confluence"

Manchester Poetry Prize – "The story starts like this: with scraps of shell," "Rally at the Capitol," "Learning the Plum Pit Game," "A Lesson in Word Choice"

The Nashville Review – "We don't know yet the little girl is safe"

The Offing – "By the Numbers 1," "By the Numbers 2," "By the Numbers 3"

Palette Poetry – "There are no police in this poem"

Pleiades – "Očhéthi, the day after the clearing of Treaty Camp"

Prairie Schooner – "Standing Rock Nocturne"

River Styx – "Thanksgiving"

Sixth Finch – "Woman Charged with Attempted Murder of Law Enforcement Officer"

Southern Humanities Review – "On Building a School"

Zócalo Public Square – "August at Očhéthi"

⬥ ⬥ ⬥

"There are no police in this poem" was the winner of the 2020 Palette Poetry Contest (Judge: Forrest Gander)

"The story starts like this: with scraps of shell," "Rally at the Capitol," "Learning the Plum Pit Game," "A Lesson in Word Choice" were short-listed for the 2020 Manchester Poetry Prize (Final judge: Malika Booker)

"On Building a School" was awarded the 2018 Auburn Witness Poetry Prize (Judge: Camille Dungy)

"We End Up at a Buffalo Butchering After the Halloween Party" was selected for Best New Poets 2018 (Judge: Kyle Dargan)

"If you're married, why do you call her Teresa?" was awarded 2nd place for the Poetry School's Gingko Ecopoetry Contest (Judges: Mimi Khalvati and Alys Fowler). "Confluence" was chosen as a highly commended poem.

"Baking Bread as Očhéthi Šakówiŋ is Raided" was awarded the 2018 *Academy of American Poets* Marion Zulauf Prize (Judge: Sarah McCartt-Jackson)

"Confluence" was reprinted in the upcoming anthology of eco-poetry, *Out of Time* (Valley Press, UK)

Personal Acknowledgements

If a book is a thing that grows, the soil that grew every bit of this book is community. Where would these words be without the love and teaching I've received from so many people? Where would I be?

First of course, the kids. Tashubi, Kenji, Kingston, Frankie, Shaylena, Shelby, Shawnee Rae, RJ, Michael, Leighton, Cheri, Bella, Mato, Eagle, Wolf, Junior, Hashtola, Alittie, TatankaSkaWin "Treyn" Swiftbird, and so many more. If you were at the school even a day, you were a part of our family. Thank you for all the joy and jokes and campfires and tears and insight and songs and much-needed hair brushing. You are so powerful. What I know of how to see a river is from you.

Alayna, can you believe that your vision created so much? That so much continues to grow from what you started in the tiny back corner of the Veteran's tent one hot day in August? You have nurtured so much beauty.

José and Blaze. Thank you for dreaming and crying and eating uncountable Nutella and peanut butter tortillas together. Your love for the kids and the school inspired me every day. I miss you when I don't know where you are.

Mama Val Eagle Shield and Lala John! Thank you for being my Standing Rock parents and taking care of me in every imaginable way—you housed me and fed me, made me feel loved, and pulled my car out of the ditch approximately one million times. There are no thank you's big enough for your love. Thank you also to Val for this incredible cover. I can't imagine anything more meaningful to me than having your art as a part of this book.

Mel Martinez, "Little" Mel Martinez, Halle Martinez, Red Rock Perkins, Kyyalyn, Waaruxti, Daniel, and Palani—thank you for being family, for caring for me and inspiring me in more ways than I can count.

Kimimila Locke, sister. My collaborator in so many things. Creating and building with you has been one of my great joys.

Leksi Steve Tamayo, you share your deep and brilliant knowledge with infinite love and generosity and we are all better for it.

Zintkala and Geneva. Your sisterhood saved me so many days. Thank you for the space you held in the glow of your fire, love, and conviction.

Savannah Begay, you brought so much light everywhere you went. You were brilliant at teaching and even more brilliant at making the kids (and me) feel safe and loved. I miss your songs and your kindness and your smile so much.

Travis, I can't believe we'll never hear you sing "NoDapl Girls" again. You gave so much time to the kids and the school wouldn't have been what it was without your big energy and enthusiasm and care.

To so many others at camp, more than I could even name, who gave me support and love and community at camp—Amber, Candy, Travis Harden, Winona Kasto, Johnnie, Sonny, Ricardo Cate, Red Fawn, Bugz, Alex Rain, Teri, Lavinia, Sonny, Tonia, JR American Horse, Jumping Buffalo, Kei, Lavinia, Sonya Smith, Wasté Win, EJ Sweetly, Elizabeth, Billy, and the Malsen family. Thank you too, to all the youth runners and Standing Rock activists who first stood up for the water and created this incredible movement. You have changed the world.

The Defenders of the Water brought so much strength to our team. Especially, thank you to Sandy Grande for your sisterhood and brilliance. You teach me so much about working toward change with community and love.

To the current Mni Wičhóni Nakíčižiŋ Wounspe team—you all inspire me every day! Memorie and Hoksila White Mountain, you are hilarious and steady and build community with the greatest hearts. Sunshine Claymore, you make everything bloom—your knowledge and care are as bright as your name.

I have been lucky enough to have such brilliant and kind teachers. I am so grateful to Allison Joseph and the late Jon Tribble. I learned so much from your teamwork. Jon's commitment to detail, passion for poetry, and constant kindness meant so much for me. Judy Jordan, when I called to tell you I was thinking of staying at the Standing Rock, you supported me and told me that you would figure out how to make my MFA work. You taught me to write and looked at at least seven versions of this book. This book would not exist without you. Jennifer Key, thank you for being a brilliant teacher as well as the kindest and funniest cheerleader a girl could ask for. Lynn Melnick, Ross Gay, Jay Desphande, Josh Edwards, Valerie Wallace—thank you for your brilliance and belief. To my high school teachers, who taught me about contemporary poetry and that being a POET was a thing a person could do—Anderson, Devaud, Romano, Brewner, Mungai, and Sampson.

Thank you so much to Tyehimba Jess, for selecting this book for the Dorset Prize. Your work has been such an inspiration and teacher to me. Thank you to Jeffrey, David, Kristina, and all the folks at Tupelo for the beautiful work you do and for ushering this book into the world. To so many friends, who have cared for me and this book along the way. Anna Leigh Knowles and Meghann Plunkett, thank you for being on this book journey together and for all of your brilliance and care. John McCarthy, Drew Hemmert, Laura Ruffino—thank you for reading a million drafts of this along the way. Jessica Lynn Suchon and Lizzy Petersen, you are my poetry soulmates. Drew Dowell, Steph Chung, Constance Parng, Evan McLaughlin, Audrey Liquard, Sarah Kock, Kate Haswell, Marian Katz, Anne Schwalbe, Andrew and Lindsey Willis Hays, Zach Simmons, Roshni Patel, Kait Walser, Sarah Jordan, and Tracy Tong—thank you for all the light you bring to me. Caitlin Barlow—I'm grateful every day for the adventure of our friendship and for your giant heart!

I wrote this book while I was pregnant and revised it with a young child and often without consistent childcare. This book would not exist without the people who made my child feel safe and loved and by extension made me feel safe and loved. Thank you especially to Emily Folk.

Thank you to Grove East Provisions, Kitchen House Coffee, and Mokabe's where much of this book was drafted. Thank you to Ida and everyone at Hungarian Pastry Shop who brought me water while I nursed, held my baby while I peed, and kept me feeling human during those early days.

A giant thank you to Shelly Smith, Jeremy Drelich, Hannah Smith-Drelich, Miriam Smith-Drelich, Martin House, and Jake Lane. I'm so lucky to join such a family filled with so much love, creativity, and intellect. Thank you also for all of the childcare help that supported the writing of this book!

Grandma, I learned so much about storytelling and love from you (and your cookies sustained more than one writing session). I miss you every day.

Mom and Dad, you read to me every night and taught me to love words. You've always encouraged my writing and not even once have you told me to do something practical instead. You've supported me in so many millions of ways and I'm so lucky to be your daughter. To my whole big loud and joyful family—I'm so lucky to have always been surrounded by love and stories.

Noah, when I said I wanted to really try to be a poet, you said, let's figure out how to do it! When I said I was thinking of staying at Očhéthi Šakówiŋ camp, you supported me and even joined me. Your steadfast love and care and humor and brilliance sustain my heart and my dreams. You keep every light on. Ira, I wrote this book while pregnant with you and revised it with you so often in my arms. You are there in every word.